WISE QUOTES: EPICTETUS

(294 EPICTETUS QUOTES)

Vol. 1 – 3

Rowan Stevens

A city is not adorned by external things, but by the virtue of those who dwell in it.

A guide, on finding a man who has lost his way, brings him back to the right path—he does not mock and jeer at him and then take himself off. You also must show the unlearned man the truth, and you will see that he will follow. But so long as you do not show it him, you should not mock, but rather feel your own incapacity.

A ship should not ride on a single anchor, nor life on a single hope.

Above all, remember that the door stands open. Be not more fearful than children; but as they, when they weary of the game, cry, I will play no more, even so, when thou art in the like case, cry, I will play no more and depart. But if thou stayest, make no lamentation.

Adopt new habits yourself: consolidate your principles by putting them into practice.

An ignorant person is inclined to blame others for his own misfortune. To blame oneself is proof of progress. But the wise man never has to blame another or himself.

An uninstructed person will lay the fault of his own bad condition upon others. Someone just starting instruction will lay the fault on himself. Some who is perfectly instructed will place blame neither on others nor on himself.

And what else can I do, lame old man that I am, than sing the praise of God? If I were a nightingale, I would perform the work of a nightingale, and if I were a swan, that of a swan. But as it is, I am a rational being, and I must sing the praise of God.

This is my work, and I accomplish it, and I will never abandon my post for as long as it is granted to me to remain in it; and I invite all of you to join me in this same song.

And where there is ignorance, there is also want of learning and instruction in essentials.

Another person will not hurt you without your cooperation; you are hurt the moment you believe yourself to be.

Any person capable of angering you becomes your master; he can anger you only when you permit yourself to be disturbed by him.

Anytus and Melitus may put me to death: to injure me is beyond their power.

If such be the will of God, so let it be.

Appearances to the mind are of four kinds. Things either are what they appear to be; or they neither are, nor appear to be; or they are, and do not appear to be; or they are not, and yet appear to be. Rightly to aim in all these cases is the wise man's task.

As a man, casting off worn out garments taketh new ones, so the dweller in the body, entereth into ones that are new.

As for us, we behave like a herd of deer. When they flee from the huntsman's feathers in affright, which way do they turn? What haven of safety do they make for? Why, they rush upon the nets! And thus they perish by confounding what they should fear with that wherein no danger lies... Not death or pain is to be feared, but the fear of death or pain. Well said the poet therefore:—Death has no terror; only a Death of shame!

As the sun does not wait for prayers and incantations to be induced to rise, but immediately shines and is saluted by all, so do you also not wait for clappings of hands and shouts of praise to be induced to do good, but be a doer of good voluntarily and you will be beloved as much as the sun.

Asked how a man should best grieve his enemy, Epictetus replied, 'By setting himself to live the noblest life himself.'

Asked, 'Who is the rich man?' Epictetus replied, 'He who is content.'

Attach yourself to what is spiritually superior, regardless of what other people think or do. Hold to your true aspirations no matter what is going on around you.

Aye, but to debase myself thus were unworthy of me. That, said Epictetus, is for you to consider, not for me. You know yourself what you are worth in your own eyes; and at what price you will sell yourself. For men sell themselves at various prices. This was why, when Florus was deliberating whether he should appear at Nero's shows, taking part in the performance himself, Agrippinus replied, 'But why do not you appear?' he answered, 'Because I do not even consider the question.' For the man who has once stooped to consider such questions, and to reckon up the value of external things, is not far from forgetting what manner of man he is. Why, what is it that you ask me? Is death preferable, or life? I reply, Life. Pain or pleasure? I reply, Pleasure. Well, but if I do not act, I shall lose my head. Then go and act! But for my part I will not act. Why? Because you think yourself but one among the many threads which make up the texture of the doublet. You should aim at being like men in general—just as your thread has no ambition either to be anything distinguished compared with the other threads. But I desire to be the purple—that small and shining part which makes the rest seem fair and beautiful. Why then do you bid me become even as the multitude? Then were I no longer the purple.

Be free from grief not through insensibility like the irrational animals, nor through want of thought like the foolish, but like a man of virtue by having reason as the consolation of grief.

Be happy when you find that doctrines you have learned and analysed are being tested by real events. If you've succeeded in removing or reducing the tendency to be mean and critical, or thoughtless, or foul-mouthed, or careless, or nonchalant; if old interests no longer engage you, at least not to the same extent; then every day can be a feast day – today because you acquitted yourself well in one set of circumstances, tomorrow because of another.

But to be hanged—is that not unendurable? Even so, when a man feels that it is reasonable, he goes off and hangs himself.

Caretake this moment. Immerse yourself in its particulars. Respond to this person, this challenge, this deed. Quit evasions. Stop giving yourself needless trouble. It is time to really live; to fully inhabit the situation you happen to be in now.

Caretake this moment. Immerse yourself in its particulars. Respond to this person, this challenge, this deed. Quit the evasions. Stop giving yourself needless trouble. It is time to really live; to fully inhabit the situation you happen to be in now. You are not some disinterested bystander. Participate. Exert yourself.

Circumstances do not rise to meet our expectations. Events happen as they do. People behave as they are. Embrace what you actually get.

Circumstances don't make the man, they only reveal him to himself.

Concerning the Gods, there are those who deny the very existence of the Godhead; others say that it exists, but neither bestirs nor concerns itself not has forethought far anything. A third party attribute to it existence and forethought, but only for great and heavenly matters, not for anything that is on earth. A fourth party admit things on earth as well as in heaven, but only in general, and not with respect to each individual. A fifth, of whom were Ulysses and Socrates, are those that cry: --I move not without Thy knowledge!

Conduct yourself in all matters, grand and public or small and domestic, in accordance with the laws of nature.

Harmonizing your will with nature should be your utmost ideal.

Control thy passions lest they take vengeance on thee.

Crows pick out the eyes of the dead, when the dead have no longer need of them; but flatterers mar the soul of the living, and her eyes they blind.

Death is not dreadful or else it would have appeared dreadful to Socrates.

!

Demand not that events should happen as you wish; but wish them to happen as they do happen, and you will go on well.

Demand not that things happen as you wish, but wish them to happen as they do, and you will go on well.

Difficulty shows what men are.

Difficulty shows what men are. Therefore when a difficulty falls upon you, remember that God, like a trainer of wrestlers, has matched you with a rough young man. Why? So that you may become an Olympic conqueror; but it is not accomplished without sweat.

Disease is an impediment to the body, but not to the will, unless the will itself chooses. Lameness is an impediment to the leg, but not to the will. And add this reflection on the occasion of everything that happens; for you will find it an impediment to something else, but not to yourself.

Do not afflict others with anything that you yourself would not wish to suffer. if you would not like to be a slave, make sure no one is your slave. If you have slaves, you yourself are the greatest slave, for just as freedom is incompatible with slavery, so goodness is incompatible with hypocrisy.

Do not decorate the walls of your house with the valuable stones from Eubœa and Sparta; but adorn the minds of the citizens and of those who administer the state with the instruction which comes from Hellas. For states are well governed by the wisdom of men, but not by stone and wood.

Do not get too attached to life for it is like a sailor's leave on the shore and at any time, the captain may sound the horn, calling you back to eternal darkness.

Do not seek for things to happen the way you want them to; rather, wish that what happens happen the way it happens: then you will be happy.

Do not try to seem wise to others. If you want to live a wise life, live it on your own terms and in your own eyes.

Does anyone bathe hastily? Do not say that they do it ill, but hastily. Does anyone drink much wine? Do not say that they do ill, but that they drink a great deal. For unless you perfectly understand their motives, how should you know if they act ill? Thus you will not risk yielding to any appearances except those you fully comprehend.

Don't concern yourself with other people's business. It's his problem if he receives you badly. And you cannot suffer for another person's fault. So don't worry about the behavior of other.

Don't explain your philosophy. Embody it.

Don't hope that events will turn out the way you want, welcome events in whichever way they happen: this is the path to peace.

Don't just say you have read books. Show that through them you have learned to think better, to be a more discriminating and reflective person. Books are the training weights of the mind. They are very helpful, but it would be a bad mistake to suppose that one has made progress simply by having internalized their contents.

Don't live by your own rules, but in harmony with nature.

Don't put your purpose in one place and expect to see progress made somewhere else.

Don't seek to have events happen as you wish, but wish them to happen as they do happen, and all will be well with you.

Don't explain your philosophy. Embody it.

Don't seek that all that comes about should come about as you wish, but wish that everything that comes about should come about just as it does, and then you'll have a calm and happy life.

Don't you want to be free of all that? 'But how can I do it?' You've often heard how – you need to suspend desire completely, and train aversion only on things within your power. You should dissociate yourself from everything outside yourself – the body, possessions, reputation, books, applause, as well as office or lack of office. Because a preference for any of them immediately makes you a slave, a subordinate, and prone to disappointment.

Either God wants to abolish evil, and cannot; or he can, but does not want to.

Even as the Sun doth not wait for prayers and incantations to rise, but shines forth and is welcomed by all: so thou also wait not for clapping of hands and shouts and praise to do thy duty; nay, do good of thine own accord, and thou wilt be loved like the Sun.

Events do not just happen, but arrive by appointment.

Every circumstance comes with two handles, which one of which you can hold it, while with the other conditions are insupportable.

Everyone's life is a warfare, and that long and various.

Faced with pain, you will discover the power of endurance. If you are insulted, you will discover patience. In time, you will grow to be confident that there is not a single impression that you will not have the moral means to tolerate.

Finally, when he crowns it off by becoming a senator, then he becomes a slave in fine company, then he experiences the poshest and most prestigious form of enslavement.

First learn the meaning of what you say, and then speak.

First say to yourself what you would be, and then do what you have to do.

First to those universal principles I have spoken of: these you must keep at command, and without them neither sleep nor rise, drink nor eat nor deal with men: the principle that no one can control another's will, and that the will alone is the sphere of good and evil.

For even sheep do not vomit up their grass and show to the shepherds how much they have eaten; but when they have internally digested the pasture, they produce externally wool and milk. Do you also show not your theorems to the uninstructed, but show the acts which come from their digestion.

For I am not Eternity, but a human being—a part of the whole, as an hour is part of the day. I must come like the hour, and like the hour must pass!

For if we had any sense, what else should we do, both in public and in private, than sing hymns and praise the deity, and recount all the favours that he has conferred!

For in this Case, we are not to give Credit to the Many, who say, that none ought to be educated but the Free; but rather to the Philosophers, who say, that the Well-educated alone are free.

For it is indeed pointless and foolish to seek to get from another what one can get from oneself. Since I can get greatness of soul and nobility of mind from myself, shall I seek to get a patch of land from you, or a bit of money, or some public post? Heaven forbid! I won't overlook my own resources in such a manner. But if someone is abject and cowardly, what on earth can one do for him except write letters for him as though on behalf of a corpse, 'Do please grant us the corpse of this man and a pint of his miserable blood'; for in truth such a person is merely a corpse and a pint of blood, and nothing more. If he amounted to anything more, he would realize that no one suffers misfortune because of the actions of another.

For it is not death or pain that is to be feared, but the fear of pain or death.

For sheep don't throw up the grass to show the shepherds how much they have eaten; but, inwardly digesting their food, they outwardly produce wool and milk. Thus, therefore, do you likewise not show theorems to the unlearned, but the actions produced by them after they have been digested.

For what else is tragedy than the portrayal in tragic verse of the sufferings of men who have attached high value to external things?

For where you find unrest, grief, fear, frustrated desire, failed aversion, jealousy and envy, happiness has no room for admittance. And where values are false, these passions inevitably follow.

Fortify yourself with contentment for this is an impregnable fortress.

Free is the person who lives as he wishes and cannot be coerced, impeded or compelled, whose impulses cannot be thwarted, who always gets what he desires and never has to experience what he would rather avoid.

Freedom is not procured by a full enjoyment of what is desired, but by controlling the desire.

Freedom is the only worthy goal in life. It is won by disregarding things that lie beyond our control.

Friend, lay hold with a desperate grasp, ere it is too late, on Freedom, on Tranquility, on Greatness of soul!

Give me by all means the shorter and nobler life, instead of one that is longer but of less account!

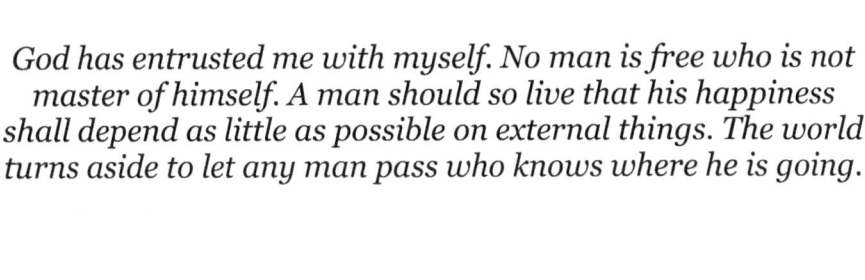

God has entrusted me with myself. No man is free who is not master of himself. A man should so live that his happiness shall depend as little as possible on external things. The world turns aside to let any man pass who knows where he is going.

God save me from fools with a little philosophy—no one is more difficult to reach.

Happiness and freedom begin with a clear understanding of one principle: Some things are within our control, and some things are not.

He did not say, 'Define me envy', and then, when the man defined it, 'You define it ill, for the terms of the definition do not correspond to the subject defined.' Such phrases are technical and therefore tiresome to the lay mind, and hard to follow, yet you and I cannot get away from them. We are quite unable to rouse the ordinary man's attention in a way which will enable him to follow his own impressions and so arrive at admitting or rejecting this or that. And therefore those of us who are at all cautious naturally give the subject up, when we become aware of this incapacity; while the mass of men, who venture at random into this sort of enterprise, muddle others and get muddled themselves, and end by abusing their opponents and getting abused in return, and so leave the field. But the first quality of all in Socrates, and the most characteristic, was that he never lost his temper in argument, never uttered anything abusive, never anything insolent, but bore with abuse from others and quieted strife.

He is a wise man who does not grieve for the things which he has not, but rejoices for those which he has.

He wants what he cannot have, and does not want what he can't refuse — and isn't aware of it. He doesn't know the difference between his own possessions and others'. Because, if he did, he would never be thwarted of disappointed. Or nervous.

He who exercises wisdom, exercises the knowledge which is about God.

He who is discontented with what he has, and with what has been granted to him by fortune, is one who is ignorant of the art of living, but he who bears that in a noble spirit, and makes reasonable use of all that comes from it, deserves to be regarded as a good man.

He who laughs at himself never runs out of things to laugh at.

Here are thieves and robbers and tribunals: and they that are called tyrants, who deem that they have after a fashion power over us, because of the miserable body and what appertains to it. Let us show them that they have power over none.

How long are you going to wait before you demand the best for yourself and in no instance bypass the discriminations of reason? You have been given the principles that you ought to endorse, and you have endorsed them. What kind of teacher, then, are you still waiting for in order to refer your self-improvement to him? You are no longer a boy, but a full-grown man. If you are careless and lazy now and keep putting things off and always deferring the day after which you will attend to yourself, you will not notice that you are making no progress, but you will live and die as someone quite ordinary.

From now on, then, resolve to live as a grown-up who is making progress, and make whatever you think best a law that you never set aside. And whenever you encounter anything that is difficult or pleasurable, or highly or lowly regarded, remember that the contest is now: you are at the Olympic Games, you cannot wait any longer, and that your progress is wrecked or preserved by a single day and a single event. That is how Socrates fulfilled himself by attending to nothing except reason in everything he encountered. And you, although you are not yet a Socrates, should live as someone who at least wants to be a Socrates.

I cannot call somebody 'hard-working' knowing only that they read and write. Even if 'all night long' is added, I cannot say it – not until I know the focus of all this energy.

I have learned to see that whatever comes about is nothing to me if it lies beyond the sphere of choice.

I laugh at those who think they can damage me. They do not know who I am, they do not know what I think, they cannot even touch the things which are really mine and with which I live.

I must die. Must I then die lamenting? I must be put in chains. Must I then also lament? I must go into exile. Does any man then hinder me from going with smiles and cheerfulness and contentment?

I want to die, even though I don't have to.

If a man has reported to you, that a certain person speaks ill of you, do not make any defense to what has been told you: but reply, The man did not know the rest of my faults, for he would not have mentioned these only.

If a person gave your body to any stranger he met on his way, you would certainly be angry. And do you feel no shame in handing over your own mind to be confused and mystified by anyone who happens to verbally attack you?

If any be unhappy, let him remember that he is unhappy by reason of himself alone. For God hath made all men to enjoy felicity and constancy of good.

If anyone tells you that a certain person speaks ill of you, do not make excuses about what is said of you but answer, He was ignorant of my other faults, else he would not have mentioned these alone.

If evil be said of thee, and if it be true, correct thyself; if it be a lie, laugh at it.

If someone speaks badly of you, do not defend yourself against the accusations, but reply; you obviously don't know about my other vices, otherwise you would have mentioned these as well

If they are wise, do not quarrel with them; if they are fools, ignore them.

If thy brother wrongs thee, remember not so much his wrong-doing, but more than ever that he is thy brother.

If what philosophers say of the kinship of God and Man be true, what remains for men to do but as Socrates did:—never, when asked one's country, to answer, I am an Athenian or a Corinthian, but I am a citizen of the world.

If you are told that such an one speaks ill of you, make no defense against what was said, but answer, He surely knows not my other faults, else he would not have mentioned these only!

If you choose, you are free; if you choose, you need blame no man—accuse no man. All things will be at once according to your mind and according to the Mind of God.

If you decide to do something, don't shrink from being seen doing it, even if the majority of people disapprove. If you're wrong to do it, then you should shrink from doing it altogether; but if you're right, then why worry how people will judge you?

If you ever happen to turn your attention to externals, for the pleasure of any one, be assured that you have ruined your scheme of life. Be contented, then, in everything, with being a philosopher; and if you wish to seem so likewise to any one, appear so to yourself, and it will suffice you.

If you have an earnest desire towards philosophy, prepare yourself from the very first to have the multitude laugh and sneer, and say, He is returned to us a philosopher all at once; and Whence this supercilious look? Now, for your part, do not have a supercilious look indeed; but keep steadily to those things which appear best to you, as one appointed by God to this particular station. For remember that, if you are persistent, those very persons who at first ridiculed will afterwards admire you. But if you are conquered by them, you will incur a double ridicule.

If you have assumed a character beyond your strength, you have both played a poor figure in that, and neglected one that is within your powers.

If you must be affected by other people's misfortunes, show them pity instead of contempt. Drop this readiness to hate and take offence.

If you pin your hopes on things outside your control, taking upon yourself things which rightfully belong to others, you are liable to stumble, fall, suffer, and blame both gods and men. But if you focus your attention only on what is truly your own concern, and leave to others what concerns them, then you will be in charge of your interior life. No one will be able to harm or hinder you. You will blame no one, and have no enemies.

If you seek Truth, you will not seek to gain a victory by every possible means; and when you have found Truth, you need not fear being defeated.

If you want to improve, be content to be thought foolish and stupid with regard to external things. Don't wish to be thought to know anything; and even if you appear to be somebody important to others, distrust yourself. For, it is difficult to both keep your faculty of choice in a state conformable to nature, and at the same time acquire external things. But while you are careful about the one, you must of necessity neglect the other.

If you wish it, you are free; if you wish it, you'll find fault with no one, you'll cast blame on no one, and everything that comes about will do so in accordance with your own will and that of God.

If you wish to be a writer, write.

If you wish to be good, first believe that you are bad.

If you wish your house to be well managed, imitate the Spartan Lycurgus. For as he did not fence his city with walls, but fortified the inhabitants by virtue and preserved the city always free; so do you not cast around (your house) a large court and raise high towers, but strengthen the dwellers by good-will and fidelity and friendship, and then nothing harmful will enter it, not even if the whole band of wickedness shall array itself against it.

If you would be a reader, read; if a writer, write.

If you would cure anger, do not feed it. Say to yourself: 'I used to be angry every day; then every other day; now only every third or fourth day.' When you reach thirty days offer a sacrifice of thanksgiving to the gods.

If, on the other hand, we read books entitled On Impulse not just out of idle curiosity, but in order to exercise impulse correctly; books entitled On Desire and On Aversion so as not to fail to get what we desire or fall victim to what we would rather avoid; and books entitled On Moral Obligation in order to honour our relationships and never do anything that clashes or conflicts with this principle; then we wouldn't get frustrated and grow impatient with our reading. Instead we would be satisfied to act accordingly. And rather than reckon, as we are used to doing, 'How many lines I read, or wrote, today,' we would pass in review how 'I applied impulse today the way the philosophers recommend.

Imagine for yourself a character, a model personality, whose example you determine to follow, in private as well as in public.

In banquets remember that you entertain two guests, body and soul: and whatever you shall have given to the body you soon eject: but what you shall have given to the soul, you keep always.

In literature, too, it is not great achievement to memorize what you have read while not formulating an opinion of your own.

In short, we do not abandon any discipline for despair of ever being the best in it.

Is freedom anything else than the right to live as we wish? Nothing else.

Is then the fruit of a fig-tree not perfect suddenly and in one hour, and would you possess the fruit of a man's mind in so short a time and so easily?

Is this all the habit you acquired when you studied philosophy, to look to others and to hope for nothing from yourself and your own acts? Lament therefore and mourn, and when you eat be fearful that you will have nothing to eat to-morrow. Tremble for your wretched slaves, lest they should steal, or run away, or die. Live in this spirit, and never cease to live so, you who never came near philosophy, except in name, and disgraced its principles so far as in you lies, by showing them to be useless and unprofitable to those who take them up.

Are you naturally entitled, then, to a good father? No, only to a father.

*Isn't reading a kind of preparation for life?
But life is composed of things other than books. It is as if an athlete, on entering the stadium, were to complain that he's not outside exercising. This was the goal of your exercise, of your weights, your practice ring and your training partners.*

It has been ordained that there be summer and winter, abundance and dearth, virtue and vice, and all such opposites for the harmony of the whole, and Zeus has given each of us a body, property, and companions.

It is a universal law — have no illusion — that every creature alive is attached to nothing so much as to its own self-interest.

It is always our choice whether or not we wish to pay the price for life's rewards. And often it is best for us not to pay the price, for the price might be our integrity.

It is better to die of hunger having lived without grief and fear, than to live with a troubled spirit, amid abundance.

It is better to do wrong seldom and to own it, and to act right for the most part, than seldom to admit that you have done wrong and to do wrong often.

It is impossible for a man to learn what he thinks he already knows.

It is more necessary for the soul to be cured than the body; for it is better to die than to live badly.

It is much better to die of hunger unhindered by grief and fear than to live affluently beset with worry, dread, suspicion and unchecked desire.

It is not events that disturb people, it is their judgements concerning them.

It is not so much what happens to you as how you think about what happens.

It is one thing to put bread and wine away in a store-room, and quite another to eat them. What is eaten is digested and distributed around the body, to become sinews, flesh, bones, blood, a good complexion, sound breathing. What is stored away is ready at hand, to be sure, to be taken out and displayed whenever you wish, but you derive no benefit from it, except that of having the reputation of possessing it.

It is our attitude toward events, not events themselves, which we can control. Nothing is by its own nature calamitous -- even death is terrible only if we fear it.

It is the act of an ill-instructed man to blame others for his own bad condition; it is the act of one who has begun to be instructed, to lay blame on himself; and of one whose instruction is completed, neither to blame another, nor himself.

It is the act of an ill-instructed man to blame others for his own bad condition; it is the act of one who has begun to be instructed, to lay the blame on himself; and of one whose instruction is completed, neither to blame another, nor himself.

It is unrealistic to expect people to see you as you see yourself.

It isn't death, pain, exile or anything else you care to mention that accounts for the way we act, only our opinion about death, pain and the rest.

It's not what happens to you, but how you react to it that matters.

Keep the prospect of death, exile and all such apparent tragedies before you every day – especially death – and you will never have an abject thought, or desire anything to excess.

Know you not that a good man does nothing for appearance sake, but for the sake of having done right?

Know, first, who you are, and then adorn yourself accordingly.

Let silence be your general rule; or say only what is necessary and in few words.

Let your will to avoid have no concern with what is not in man's power; direct it only to things in man's power that are contrary to nature.

Lucky is the man who dies at work.

Man is not worried by real problems so much as by his imagined anxieties about real problems

Man, what are you talking about? Me in chains? You may fetter my leg but my will, not even Zeus himself can overpower.

Many people who have progressively lowered their personal standards in an attempt to win social acceptance and life's comforts bitterly resent those of philosophical bent who refuse to compromise their spiritual ideals and who seek to better themselves.

Men are disturbed not by the things that happen, but by their opinion of the things that happen.

Men are disturbed not by things, but by the views which they take of things. Thus death is nothing terrible, else it would have appeared so to Socrates. But the terror consists in our notion of death, that it is terrible. When, therefore, we are hindered, or disturbed, or grieved let us never impute it to others, but to ourselves; that is, to our own views. It is the action of an uninstructed person to reproach others for his own misfortunes; of one entering upon instruction, to reproach himself; and of one perfectly instructed, to reproach neither others or himself.

Most of what passes for legitimate entertainment is inferior or foolish and only caters to or exploits people's weaknesses. Avoid being one of the mob who indulges in such pastimes. Your life is too short and you have important things to do. Be discriminating about what images and ideas you permit into your mind. If you yourself don't choose what thoughts and images you expose yourself to, someone else will, and their motives may not be the highest. It is the easiest thing in the world to slide imperceptibly into vulgarity. But there's no need for that to happen if you determine not to waste your time and attention on mindless pap.

Most people are impulsive, however, and having committed to the thing, they persist, just making more confusion for themselves and others until it all end in mutual recrimination.

Nature hath given men one tongue but two ears, that we may hear from others twice as much as we speak.

Neither should a ship rely on one small anchor, nor should life rest on a single hope.

Never depend on the admiration of others. There is no strength in it. Personal merit cannot be derived from an external source. It is not to be found in your personal associations, nor can it be found in the regard of other people. It is a fact of life that other people, even people who love you, will not necessarily agree with your ideas, understand you, or share your enthusiasms. Grow up! Who cares what other people think about you!

Never praise or blame people on common grounds; look to their judgements exclusively. Because that is the determining factor, which makes everyone's actions either good or bad.

Never say about anything, I have lost it, but only I have given it back.

No great thing is created suddenly, any more than a bunch of grapes or a fig. If you tell me that you desire a fig, I answer that there must be time. Let it first blossom, then bear fruit, then ripen.

No man is free until he is a master of himself.

No one is ever unhappy because of someone else.

None of these things are foretold to me; but either to my paltry body, or property, or reputation, or children, or wife. But to me all omens are lucky, if I will. For whichever of these things happens, it is in my control to derive advantage from it.

Nothing great comes into being all at once, for that is not the case even with a bunch of grapes or a fig. If you tell me now, 'I want a fig,' I'll reply, 'That takes time.

Nothing important comes into being overnight; even grapes and figs need time to ripen. If you say that you want a fig now, I will tell you to be patient. First, you must allow the tree to flower, then put forth fruit; then you have to wait until the fruit is ripe. So if the fruit of a fig tree is not brought to maturity instantly or in an hour, how do you expect the human mind to come to fruition, so quickly and easily?

Now is the time to get serious about living your ideals. How long can you afford to put off who you really want to be? Your nobler self cannot wait any longer. Put your principles into practice – now. Stop the excuses and the procrastination. This is your life! You aren't a child anymore. The sooner you set yourself to your spiritual program, the happier you will be. The longer you wait, the more you'll be vulnerable to mediocrity and feel filled with shame and regret, because you know you are capable of better. From this instant on, vow to stop disappointing yourself. Separate yourself from the mob. Decide to be extraordinary and do what you need to do – now.

Now there are two kinds of hardening, one of the understanding, the other of the sense of shame, when a man is resolved not to assent to what is manifest nor to desist from contradictions. Most of us are afraid of mortification of the body, and would contrive all means to avoid such a thing, but we care not about the soul's mortification. And indeed with regard to the soul, if a man be in such a state as not to apprehend anything, or understand at all, we think that he is in a bad condition; but if the sense of shame and modesty are deadened, this we call even power or strength.

On the occasion of every event that befalls you, remember to turn to yourself and inquire what power you have for turning it to use.

Once I was liable to the same mistakes, but, thanks to God, no longer...
Well, isn't it just as worthwhile to have devoted and applied yourself to this goal as to have read or written fifty pages?

Only the educated are free.

Other people's views and troubles can be contagious. Don't sabotage yourself by unwittingly adopting negative, unproductive attitudes through your associations with others.

Our situation is like that at a festival. Sheep and cattle are driven to it to be sold, and most people come either to buy or to sell, while only a few come to look at the spectacle of the festival, to see how it is proceeding and why, and who is organizing it, and for what purpose. So also in this festival of the world. Some people are like sheep and cattle and are interested in nothing but their fodder; for in the case of those of you who are interested in nothing but your property, and land, and slaves, and public posts, all of that is nothing more than fodder. Few indeed are those who attend the fair for love of the spectacle, asking, 'What is the universe, then, and who governs it? No one at all? And yet when a city or household cannot survive for even a very short time without someone to govern it and watch over it, how could it be that such a vast and beautiful structure could be kept so well ordered by mere chance and good luck? So there must be someone governing it. What sort of being is he, and how does he govern it? And we who have been created by him, who are we, and what were we created for? Are we bound together with him in some kind of union and interrelationship, or is that not the case?' Such are the thoughts that are aroused in this small collection of people; and from then on, they devote their leisure to this one thing alone, to finding out about the festival before they have to take their leave. What comes about, then? They become an object of mockery for the crowd, just as the spectators at an ordinary festival are mocked by the traders; and even the sheep and cattle, if they had sufficient intelligence, would laugh at those who attach value to anything other than fodder!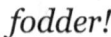

People are not disturbed by things, but by the view they take of them.

People are ready to acknowledge some of their faults, but will admit to others only with reluctance.

People find particular things, however, frightening; and it's when someone is able to threaten or entice us with those that the man himself becomes frightening.

!

People with a strong physical constitution can tolerate extremes of hot and cold; people of strong mental health can handle anger, grief, joy and the other emotions.

Philosophy does not claim to secure for us anything outside our control. Otherwise it would be taking on matters that do not concern it. For as wood is the material of the carpenter, and marble that of the sculptor, so the subject matter of the art of life is the life of the self.

Preach not to others what they should eat, but eat as becomes you and be silent.

Prefer enduring satisfaction to immediate gratification.

Protect what belongs to you at all costs; don't desire what belongs to another.

Reading should serve the goal of attaining peace; if it doesn't make you peaceful, what good is it?

Remember from now on whenever something tends to make you unhappy, draw on this principle: 'This is no misfortune; but bearing with it bravely is a blessing.

Remember that you ought to behave in life as you would at a banquet. As something is being passed around it comes to you; stretch out your hand, take a portion of it politely. It passes on; do not detain it. Or it has not come to you yet; do not project your desire to meet it, but wait until it comes in front of you. So act toward children, so toward a wife, so toward office, so toward wealth.

Remember then that if you think the things which are by nature slavish to be free, and the things which are in the power of others to be your own, you will be hindered, you will lament, you will be disturbed, you will blame both gods and men: but if you think that only which is your own to be your own, and if you think that what is another's, as it really is, belongs to another, no man will ever compel you, no man will hinder you, you will never blame any man, you will accuse no man, you will do nothing involuntarily (against your will), no man will harm you, you will have no enemy, for you will not suffer any harm.

Remember, it is not enough to be hit or insulted to be harmed, you must believe that you are being harmed. If someone succeeds in provoking you, realize that your mind is complicit in the provocation. Which is why it is essential that we not respond impulsively to impressions; take a moment before reacting, and you will find it easier to maintain control.

Remind thyself that he whom thou lovest is mortal that what thou lovest is not thine own; it is given thee for the present, not irrevocably nor forever, but even as a fig or a bunch of grapes at the appointed season of the year.

Resistance is vain in any case; it only leads to useless struggle while inviting grief and sorrow.

Restrict yourself to choice and refusal; and exercise them carefully, with discipline and detachment.

Seek not that the things which happen should happen as you wish; but wish the things which happen to be as they are, and you will have a tranquil flow of life.

Seek not the good in external things; seek it in yourselves.

Sick and yet happy, in peril and yet happy, dying and yet happy, in exile and happy, in disgrace and happy.

Sickness is a problem for the body, not the mind — unless the mind decides that it is a problem. Lameness, too, is the body's problem, not the mind's. Say this to yourself whatever the circumstance and you will find without fail that the problem pertains to something else, not to you.

Small-minded people blame others. Average people blame themselves. The wise see all blame as foolishness.

So don't make a show of your philosophical learning to the uninitiated, show them by your actions what you have absorbed.

So if you like doing something, do it regularly; if you don't like doing something, make a habit of doing something different.

So what oppresses and scares us? It is our own thoughts, obviously. What overwhelms people when they are about to leaves friends, family, old haunts and their accustomed way of life? Thoughts.

So you wish to conquer in the Olympic Games, my friend? And I, too... But first mark the conditions and the consequences. You will have to put yourself under discipline; to eat by rule, to avoid cakes and sweetmeats; to take exercise at the appointed hour whether you like it or not, in cold and heat; to abstain from cold drinks and wine at your will. Then, in the conflict itself you are likely enough to dislocate your wrist or twist your ankle, to swallow a great deal of dust, to be severely thrashed, and after all of these things, to be defeated.

Some things are in our control and others not. Things in our control are opinion, pursuit, desire, aversion, and, in a word, whatever are our own actions. Things not in our control are body, property, reputation, command, and, in one word, whatever are not our actions. The things in our control are by nature free, unrestrained, unhindered; but those not in our control are weak, slavish, restrained, belonging to others. Remember, then, that if you suppose that things which are slavish by nature are also free, and that what belongs to others is your own, then you will be hindered. You will lament, you will be disturbed, and you will find fault both with gods and men. But if you suppose that only to be your own which is your own, and what belongs to others such as it really is, then no one will ever compel you or restrain you. Further, you will find fault with no one or accuse no one. You will do nothing against your will. No one will hurt you, you will have no enemies, and you not be harmed.

Some young women confuse their self-worth with their ability to attract the attention of men, and so pour all their energies into makeup, clothing, and jewelry. If only they realized that virtue, honor, and self-respect are the marks of a true beauty.

Stop honouring externals, quit turning yourself into the tool of mere matter, or of people who can supply you or deny you those material things.

Such was, and is, and will be the nature of the universe, and it isn't possible that things should come into being in any other way than they do at present; and not only have human beings participated in the process of change and transformation along with all the other creatures that live on the earth, but also those beings that are divine, and, by Zeus, even the four elements, which are changed and transformed upwards and downwards, as earth becomes water, and water air, and air is transformed in turn into ether. If someone endeavours to turn his mind towards these things, and to persuade himself to accept of his own free will what must necessarily come about, he will live a very balanced and harmonious life.

Take care not to hurt the ruling faculty of your mind. If you were to guard against this in every action, you should enter upon those actions more safely.

Tell yourself what you want to be, then act your part accordingly.

Tentative efforts lead to tentative outcomes. Therefore, give yourself fully to your endeavors. Decide to construct your character through excellent actions and determine to pay the price of a worthy goal. The trials you encounter will introduce you to your strengths. Remain steadfast...and one day you will build something that endures: something worthy of your potential.

That is the way things are weighed and disagreements settled — when standards are established. Philosophy aims to test and set such standards. And the wise man is advised to make use of their findings right way.

The chief task in life is simply this: to identify and separate matters so that I can say clearly to myself which are externals not under my control, and which have to do with the choices I actually control. Where then do I look for good and evil? Not to uncontrollable externals, but within myself to the choices that are my own...

The condition and characteristic of an uninstructed person is this: he never expects from himself advantage nor harm, but from externals. The condition and characteristic of a philosopher is this: he expects all advantage and all harm from himself.

The essence of philosophy is that a man should so live that his happiness shall depend as little as possible on external things.

The first and most important field of philosophy is the application of principles such as Do not lie. Next come the proofs, such as why we should not lie. The third field supports and articulates the proofs, by asking, for example, How does this prove it? What exactly is a proof, what is logical inference, what is contradiction, what is truth, what is falsehood? Thus, the third field is necessary because of the second, and the second because of the first. The most important, though, the one that should occupy most of our time, is the first. But we do just the opposite. We are preoccupied with the third field and give that all our attention, passing the first by altogether. The result is that we lie – but have no difficulty proving why we shouldn't.

The gods do not exist, and even if they exist they do not trouble themselves about people, and we have nothing in common with them. The piety and devotion to the gods that the majority of people invoke is a lie devised by swindlers and con men and, if you can believe it, by legislators, to keep criminals in line by putting the fear of God into them.

The good of man, and likewise his ill, lies in how he exercises his choice, while everything else is nothing to us.

*The greater the difficulty, the more glory in surmounting it.
Skillful pilots gain their reputation from storms and tempests.*

*The husbandman deals with land; physicians and trainers
with the body; the wise man with his own Mind.*

*The key is to keep company only with people who uplift you,
whose presence calls forth your best.*

*The knowledge of what is mine and what is not mine, what I
can and cannot do. I must die. But must I die bawling? I must
be exiled; but is there anything to keep me from going with a
smile, calm and self-composed?*

The man has to learn 'what each specific thing means', as Socrates often said, and stop casually applying preconceptions to individual cases.
This is the cause of everyone's troubles, the inability to apply common preconceptions to particulars. Instead the opinions of men as to what is bad diverge.

The more we value things outside our control, the less control we have.

The philosopher's school, ye men, is a surgery: you ought not to go out of it with pleasure, but with pain. For you are not in sound health when you enter.

The soul is like the bowl of water, with the soul's impressions like the rays of light that strike the water. Now, if the water is disturbed, the light appears to be disturbed together with it — though of course it is not. So when someone loses consciousness, it is not the person's knowledge and virtues that are impaired, it is the breath that contains them. Once the breath returns to normal, knowledge and the virtues are restored to normal also.

The wise person knows it is fruitless to project hopes and fears on the future. This only leads to forming melodramatic representations in your mind and wasting time.

There is a time and place for diversion and amusements, but you should never allow them to override your true purposes.

There is but one way to tranquility of mind and happiness, and that is to account no external things thine own, but to commit all to God.

There is no shame in making an honest effort.

There is only one way to happiness and that is to cease worrying about things which are beyond the power or our will.

These reasonings are unconnected: I am richer than you, therefore I am better; I am more eloquent than you, therefore I am better. The connection is rather this: I am richer than you, therefore my property is greater than yours; I am more eloquent than you, therefore my style is better than yours. But you, after all, are neither property nor style.

This is your business—to act well the given part, but to choose it belongs to another.

Those proficient praise no one, blame no one, and accuse no one. They say nothing concerning their self as being anybody or knowing anything.

Those who are well constituted in the body endure both heat and cold: and so those who are well constituted in the soul endure both anger and grief and excessive joy and the other affects.

Tis true I know what evil I shall do but passion overpowers the better council.

To accuse others for one's own misfortune is a sign of want of education. To accuse oneself shows that one's education has begun. To accuse neither oneself nor others shows that one's education is complete.

To admonish is better than to reproach for admonition is mild and friendly, but reproach is harsh and insulting; and admonition corrects those who are doing wrong, but reproach only convicts them.

To Epictetus, all external events are determined by fate, and are thus beyond our control, but we can accept whatever happens calmly and dispassionately. Individuals, however, are responsible for their own actions which they can examine and control through rigorous self-discipline. Suffering arises from trying to control what is uncontrollable, or from neglecting what is within our power. As part of the universal city that is the universe, human beings have a duty of care to all fellow humans. The person who followed these precepts would achieve happiness.

Today, when the crisis calls you, will you go off and display your recitation and harp on, 'How cleverly I compose dialogues'? Nay, fellow man, make this your object, 'Look how I fail not to get what I will. Look how I escape what I will to avoid. Let death come and you shall know; bring me pains, prison, dishonour, condemnation.' This is the true field of display for a young man come from school. Leave those other trifles to other men; let no one ever hear you say a word on them, do not tolerate any compliments upon them; assume the air of being no one and of knowing nothing. Show that you know this only, how not to fail and how not to fall.

Understand that every event is indifferent and nothing to you, of whatever sort it may be; for it will be in your power to make a right use of it, and this no one can hinder.

Understand what words you use first, then use them.

Very little is needed for everything to be upset and ruined, only a slight lapse in reason.

We are at the mercy of whoever wields authority over the things we either desire or detest. If you would be free, then, do not wish to have, or avoid, things that other people control, because then you must serve as their slave.

We are not disturbed by what happens to us, but by our thoughts about what happens to us.

We aren't filled with fear except by things that are bad; and not by them, either, as long as it is in our power to avoid them.

We cannot choose our external circumstances, but we can always choose how we respond to them.

We have two ears and one mouth so that we can listen twice as much as we speak.

We must consider what is the time for singing, what the time for play, and in whose presence: what will be unsuited to the occasion; whether our companions are to despise us, or we to despise ourselves: when to jest, and whom to mock at: and on what occasion to be conciliatory and to whom: in a word, how one ought to maintain one's character in society. Wherever you swerve from any of these principles, you suffer loss at once; not loss from without, but issuing from the very act itself.

We must not believe the many, who say that only free people ought to be educated, but we should rather believe the philosophers who say that only the educated are free.

We should realize that an opinion is not easily formed unless a person says and hears the same things every day and practises them in real life.

Wealth consists not in having great possessions, but in having few wants.

What are we to do, then? To make the best of what lies within our power, and deal with everything else as it comes. 'How does it come, then?' As God wills.

What is death? A tragic mask. Turn it and examine it. See, it does not bite. The poor body must be separated from the spirit either now or later, as it was separated from it before. Why, then, are you troubled, if it be separated now? for if it is not separated now, it will be separated afterward. Why? That the period of the universe may be completed, for it has need of the present, and of the future, and of the past. What is pain? A mask. Turn it and examine it. The poor flesh is moved roughly, then, on the contrary, smoothly. If this does not satisfy you, the door is open: if it does, bear. For the door ought to be open for all occasions; and so we have no trouble.

What sayeth Antisthenes? Hast thou never heard?— It is a kingly thing, O Cyrus, to do well and to be evil spoken of.

What then, is it not possible to be free from faults? It is not possible; but this is possible: to direct your efforts incessantly to being faultless. For we must be content if by never remitting this attention we shall escape at least a few errors. When you have said Tomorrow I will begin to attend, you must be told that you are saying this: Today I will be shameless, disregardful of time and place, mean; it will be in the power of others to give me pain, today I will be passionate and envious.

See how many evil things you are permitting yourself to do. If it is good to use attention tomorrow, how much better is it to do so today? If tomorrow it is in your interest to attend, much more is it today, that you may be able to do so tomorrow also, and may not defer it again to the third day.

What would have become of Hercules do you think if there had been no lion, hydra, stag or boar - and no savage criminals to rid the world of? What would he have done in the absence of such challenges?

Obviously he would have just rolled over in bed and gone back to sleep. So by snoring his life away in luxury and comfort he never would have developed into the mighty Hercules.

And even if he had, what good would it have done him? What would have been the use of those arms, that physique, and that noble soul, without crises or conditions to stir into him action?

What you shun enduring yourself, attempt not to impose on others. You shun slavery- beware enslaving others! If you can endure to do that, one would think you had been once upon a time a slave yourself. For vice has nothing in common with virtue, nor Freedom with slavery.

Whatever moral rules you have deliberately proposed to yourself. abide by them as they were laws, and as if you would be guilty of impiety by violating any of them. Don't regard what anyone says of you, for this, after all, is no concern of yours.

Whatever your mission, stick by it as if it were a law and you would be committing sacrilege to betray it. Pay no attention to whatever people might say; this no longer should influence you.

When a man is proud because he can understand and explain the writings of Chrysippus, say to yourself, if Chrysippus had not written obscurely, this man would have had nothing to be proud of.

When a youth was giving himself airs in the Theatre and saying, 'I am wise, for I have conversed with many wise men,' Epictetus replied, 'I too have conversed with many rich men, yet I am not rich!'.

When any person harms you, or speaks badly of you, remember that he acts or speaks from a supposition of its being his duty. Now, it is not possible that he should follow what appears right to you, but what appears so to himself. Therefore, if he judges from a wrong appearance, he is the person hurt, since he too is the person deceived. For if anyone should suppose a true proposition to be false, the proposition is not hurt, but he who is deceived about it. Setting out, then, from these principles, you will meekly bear a person who reviles you, for you will say upon every occasion, It seemed so to him.

When someone is properly grounded in life, they shouldn't have to look outside themselves for approval.

When then any man assents to that which is false, be assured that he did not intend to assent to it as false, for every soul is unwillingly deprived of the truth, as Plato says; but the falsity seemed to him to be true.

When things seem to have reached that stage, merely say I won't play any longer, and take your departure; but if you stay, stop lamenting.

When we blather about trivial things, we ourselves become trivial, for our attention gets taken up with trivialities. You become what you give your attention to.

When you do anything from a clear judgment that it ought to be done, never shrink from being seen to do it, even though the world should misunderstand it; for if you are not acting rightly, shun the action itself; if you are, why fear those who wrongly censure you?

When you find your direction, check to make sure that it is the right one.

When, therefore, you see anyone eminent in honors, or power, or in high esteem on any other account, take heed not to be hurried away with the appearance, and to pronounce him happy; for, if the essence of good consists in things in our own control, there will be no room for envy or emulation. But, for your part, don't wish to be a general, or a senator, or a consul, but to be free;

Whenever anyone criticizes or wrongs you, remember that they are only doing or saying what they think is right. They cannot be guided by your views, only their own; so if their views are wrong, they are the ones who suffer insofar as they are misguided.

Wherever I go it will be well with me, for it was well with me here, not on account of the place, but of my judgments which I shall carry away with me, for no one can deprive me of these; on the contrary, they alone are my property, and cannot be taken away, and to possess them suffices me wherever I am or whatever I do.

Who are those people by whom you wish to be admired? Are they not these whom you are in the habit of saying that they are mad? What then? Do you wish to be admired by the mad?

Who is a friend? his answer was, an alter ego.

Who is your master? Whoever has authority over anything that you're anxious to gain or avoid.

Who then is invincible? The one who cannot be upset by anything outside their reasoned choice.

Who, then, is the invincible human being? One who can be disconcerted by nothing that lies outside the sphere of choice.

Whoever chafes at the conditions dealt by fate is unskilled in the art of life; whoever bears with them nobly and makes wise use of the results is a man who deserves to be considered good.

Whoever is going to listen to the philosophers needs a considerable practice in listening.

Whoever then would be free, let him wish for nothing, let him decline nothing, which depends on others; else he must necessarily be a slave.

Why are we not angry if we are told that we have a headache, and why are we angry if we are told that we reason badly, or choose wrongly? The reason is that we are quite certain that we have not a headache, or are not lame, but we are not so sure that we make a true choice. So having assurance only because we see with our whole sight, it puts us into suspense and surprise when another with his whole sight sees the opposite, and still more so when a thousand others deride our choice. For we must prefer our own lights to those of so many others, and that is bold and difficult.

Why do you want to read anyway – for the sake of amusement or mere erudition? Those are poor, fatuous pretexts.
Reading should serve the goal of attaining peace; if it doesn't make you peaceful, what good is it?

Yes, but my nose is running. Then what do you have hands for?

You are a little soul carrying a dead body.

You become what you give your attention to.

You journey to Olympia to see the work of Phidias; and each of you holds it a misfortune not to have beheld these things before you die. Whereas when there is no need even to take a journey, but you are on the spot, with the works before you, have you no care to contemplate and study these? Will you not then perceive either who you are or unto what end you were born: or for what purpose the power of contemplation has been bestowed on you? Well, but in life there are some things disagreeable and hard to bear. And are there none at Olympia? Are you not scorched by the heat? Are you not cramped for room? Have you not to bathe with discomfort? Are you not drenched when it rains? Have you not to endure the clamor and shouting and such annoyances as these? Well, I suppose you set all this over against the splendour of the spectacle and bear it patiently. What then? have you not received greatness of heart, received courage, received fortitude? What care I, if I am great of heart, for aught that can come to pass? What shall cast me down or disturb me? What shall seem painful? Shall I not use the power to the end for which I received it, instead of moaning and wailing over what comes to pass?

You know yourself what you are worth in your own eyes; and at what price you will sell yourself. For men sell themselves at various prices. This is why, when Florus was deliberating whether he should appear at Nero's shows, taking part in the performance himself, Agrippinus replied, 'Appear by all means.' And when Florus inquired, 'But why do not you appear?' he answered, 'Because I do not even consider the question.' For the man who has once stooped to consider such questions, and to reckon up the value of external things, is not far from forgetting what manner of man he is.

You may fetter my leg, but Zeus himself cannot get the better of my free will.

You ought to realize, you take up very little space in the world as a whole—your body, that is; in reason, however, you yield to no one, not even to the gods, because reason is not measured in size but sense. So why not care for that side of you, where you and the gods are equals?

You should be especially careful when associating with one of your former friends or acquaintances not to sink to their level; otherwise you will lose yourself. If you are troubled by the idea that 'He'll think I'm boring and won't treat me the way he used to,' remember that everything comes at a price. It isn't possible to change your behavior and still be the same person you were before.

You will do the greatest services to the state, if you shall raise not the roofs of the houses, but the souls of the citizens: for it is better that great souls should dwell in small houses than for mean slaves to lurk in great houses.

You will never have to experience defeat if you avoid contests whose outcome is outside your control.

You would fain be victor at the Olympic Games, you say. Yes, but weigh the conditions, weigh the consequences; then and then only, lay to your hand–if it be for your profit. You must live by rule, submit to diet, abstain from dainty meats, exercise your body perforce at stated hours, in heat or in cold; drink no cold water, nor, it may be, wine. In a word, you must surrender yourself wholly to your trainer, as though to a physician.

You'd have a better chance persuading someone to change their sexual orientation than reaching people who have rendered themselves so deaf and blind.

You're not yet Socrates, but you can still live as if you want to be him.

You're unable to make someone change his views, recognize that he is a child, and clap as he does. Or if you don't care to act in such a way, you have only to keep quiet.

Your happiness depends on three things, all of which are within your power: your will, your ideas concerning the events in which you are involved, and the use you make of your ideas.

www.ingramcontent.com/pod-product-compliance
Lightning Source LLC
Chambersburg PA
CBHW071252070526
44583CB00017B/2438